"I would rather die of passion than of boredom."
Vincent Van Gogh

"If you're going through hell, keep going."
Winston Churchill

"Fear, uncertainty and discomfort are your compasses toward growth."

"An essential part of creativity is not being afraid to fail."
Edwin H. Lan

"A hero is one who knows how to hang on for one minute longer."
Norwegian proverb

"The brain is like a muscle. When it is in use we
feel very good. Understanding is joyous."
Carl Sagan

"It's not what happens to you, but how you react to it that matters."
Epictetus

"Unless you try to do something beyond what you have
already mastered you will never grow."
Ralph Waldo Emerson

"Trust yourself. Create the kind of self that you
will be happy to live with all your life."
Golda Meir

"To be wronged is nothing unless you continue to remember it."
Confucius

"Winning starts with beginning."

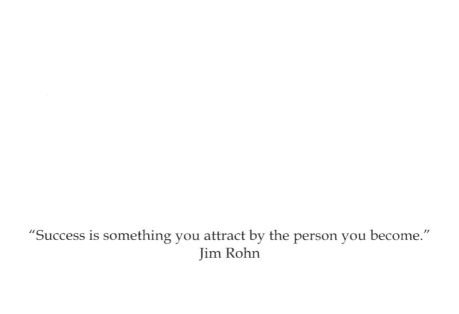
"Success is something you attract by the person you become."
Jim Rohn

"Use what talents you possess; the woods would be very silent
if no birds sang there except those that sang best."
Henry van Dyke

"The only way to do great work is to love what you do. If you haven't found it yet, keep looking. Don't settle."
Steve Jobs

"Choose a job you love and you will never have to work a day of your life."

"Inside of every problem lies an opportunity."
Robert Kiyosaki

"Don't let a bad day make you feel like you have a bad life."

"Don't let yesterday use up too much of today."
Will Rogers

"Do one thing every day that scares you."
Mary Schmich

"Showing off is the fool's idea of glory."
Bruce Lee

"Don't limit your challenges - challenge your limits."

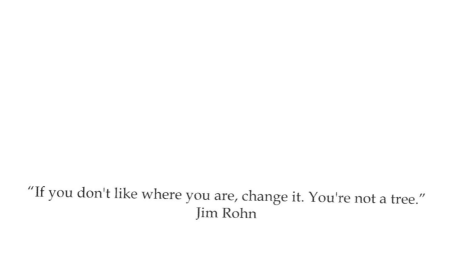

"If you don't like where you are, change it. You're not a tree."
Jim Rohn

"It is time to shed the burdens of the past year and come up fresh and alive."
Sadhguru

"Waste no more time arguing about what a good person should be.
Be one."
Marcus Aurelius

"You must expect failure as part of your journey of success, failure andsuccess go hand in hand, you cannot have one without the other."
Richard Parkes Cordock

"Always remember you are braver than you believe, stronger than you seem, and smarter than you think"
A. A. Milne

"There are always limits, and there are always opportunities. The ones we rehearse and focus on are the ones that shape our attitude and our actions."
Seth Godin

"What makes you different or weird—that's your strength."
Meryl Streep

"The longer we dwell on our misfortunes, the greater is their power to harm us."

"Hardships often prepare ordinary people for an extraordinary destiny."
C. S. Lewis

"To be yourself in a world that is constantly trying to make you something else is the greatest accomplishment."
Ralph Waldo Emerson

"Breathe. Take care. Stand still for a minute. What you are looking for might just be looking for you too."
Cleo Wade

"Be a practical dreamer, backed by action."
Bruce Lee

"We grow fearless when we do the things we fear."
Robin Sharma

"We tend to judge others by their behavior, and ourselves by our intentions."

"Ask yourself, who do you want to be? Figure out for yourself what makes you happy, no matter how crazy it may sound to other people."
Arnold Schwarzenegger

"The best way to predict the future is to create it."
Peter Drucker

"Don't think about what might go wrong, think about what could be right."

"It is no measure of health to be well adjusted to a profoundly sick society."
J. Krishnamurti

"Keep smiling, because life is a beautiful thing
and there's so much to smile about."
Marilyn Monroe

"Sometimes good things fall apart so better things can fall together."
Marilyn Monroe

"Decide that you want it more than you are afraid of it."

"You can't get much done in life if you only
work on the days when you feel good."
Jerry West

"Success isn't about how your life looks to others.
It's about how it feels to you."
Michelle Obama

"One of the greatest discoveries a person makes is to find they can do what they were afraid they couldn't do."
Henry Ford

"Happiness is a way of travel. Not a destination."
Roy Goodman

"Life shrinks or expands in proportion to your courage."
Anais Nin

"Let go of the thoughts that don't make you strong."

"The death of a dream is the day that you stop believing
in the work it takes to get there."
Chris Burkmenn

"The best teachers are those who show you where to
look, but don't tell you what to see."
Alexandra K. Trenfor

"Be who you were created to be, and you will set the world on fire."
St. Catherine of Siena

"Stay hungry; stay foolish."
Whole Earth Epilog

"Victory is always possible for the person who refuses to stop fighting."
Napoleon Hill

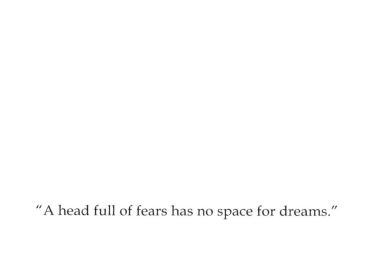

"A head full of fears has no space for dreams."

"Failure is success if you learn from it."

"The world breaks everyone and afterward many
are strong at the broken places."
Ernest Hemingway

"When you have confidence, you can have a lot of fun. And
when you have fun, you can do amazing things."
Joe Namath

"People grow through experience if they meet life honestly
and courageously. This is how character is built."
Eleanor Roosevelt

"The bigger the dream, the more important the team."
Robin Sharma

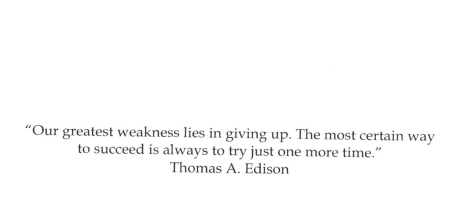
"Our greatest weakness lies in giving up. The most certain way to succeed is always to try just one more time."
Thomas A. Edison

"If you tell yourself you can't, you won't."
Dean Graziosi

"Don't let small minds convince you that your dreams are too big."

"While we are postponing, life speeds by."

"Whatever you think you can do or believe you can do, begin
it. Action has magic, grace, and power in it."
Johann Wolfgang von Goethe

"If you focus on what you left behind, then how can you see what
lies ahead?"
Chef Gusteau, "Ratatouille"

"We do not need magic to transform our world. We carry all
the power we need inside ourselves already."
J.K. Rowling

"Incredible change happens in your life when you decide to take control of what you do have power over instead of craving control over what you don't."
Steve Maraboli

"Always remember that the future comes one day at a time."
Dean Acheson

"If you don't like something, change it. If you can't change it, change your attitude. Don't complain."
Maya Angelou

"Step out of the history that is holding you back. Step into the new story you are willing to create."
Oprah Winfrey

"Follow your bliss and the universe will open
doors where there were only walls."
Joseph Campbell

"There are two primary choices in life: to accept conditions as they exist, or accept the responsibility for changing them."
Denis Waitley

"Simplicity is the ultimate sophistication."
Leonardo da Vinci

"If you want to go fast, go alone. If you want to go far, bring others along."

"Slow progress is better than no progress."

"Things may come to those who wait, but only
the things left by those who hustle."

"The privilege of a lifetime is being who you are."
Joseph Campbell

"There is never enough time to do everything, but there is always enough time to do the most important thing."
Brian Tracy

"Sometimes the questions are complicated and the answers are simple."
Dr. Seuss

"The best way to not feel hopeless is to get up and do something."
Barack Obama

"Magic is believing in yourself, if you can do
that, you can make anything happen."
Johann Wolfgang Von Goethe

"If you really believe in what you're doing, work hard, take nothing personally and if something blocks one route, find another. Never give up."
Laurie Notaro

"You don't learn to walk by following rules. You learn by doing, and by falling over."
Richard Branson

"Within you is a stillness and a sanctuary to which you
can retreat at any time and be yourself."
Hermann Hesse

"There is no such thing as failure, just lessons to be learnt on the way."
Sadhguru

"We awaken in others the same attitude of mind we hold toward them."
Elbert Hubbard

"Never underestimate your problem or your ability to deal with it."
Robert Schuller

"The world will ask you who you are, and if you
do not know, the world will tell you."
Carl Jung

"Change your life today. Don't gamble on the future, act now, without delay."
Simone de Beauvoir

"Wherever you are, be all there."
Jim Elliot

"You don't always need a plan. Sometimes you just need to breathe, trust, let go, and see what happens."
Mandy Hale

"We don't see things as they are, we see them as we are."
Anais Nin

"Don't blame others as an excuse for you not working hard
enough."

"Too many of us are not living our dreams because we are living
our fears."
Les Brown

"Expect great things, and great things will come."
Norman Vincent Peale

"Whenever you are confronted with an opponent, conquer them with love."
Mahatma Gandhi

"Jumping from failure to failure with undiminished
enthusiasm is the big secret to success."
Savas Dimopoulos

"Awareness is the greatest agent for change."
Eckhart Tolle

"Nothing diminishes anxiety faster than action."
Walter Anderson

"Courage doesn't always roar. Sometimes courage is the quiet voice at the end of the day whispering, 'I will try again tomorrow.'" Mary Anne Radmacher

"Do a little more of what you want to do every day,
until your idea becomes what's real."

"If you spend too much time thinking about a thing, you'll never get it done."
Bruce Lee

"Follow your instincts. That's where true wisdom manifests itself."
Oprah Winfrey

"The struggle you're in today is developing the strength you need for tomorrow."

"If you fell down yesterday, stand up today."
H.G. Wells

"Live in the present and make it so beautiful that it is worth remembering"

"Take care of what is big while it's still small."
Lao Tzu

Made in the USA
Coppell, TX
27 October 2024

39257203R00066